57 Piano Pieces Children Like to Play

ED. 2050

G. SCHIRMER, Inc.

DISTRIBUTED BY

HAL•LEONARD®
CORPORATION

7777 W. BLUEMOUND RD. P.O. BOX 13819 MILWAUKEE, WI 53213

ALPHABETICAL INDEX BY COMPOSER

ALPHABETICAL INDEX BY TITLE

French Child's Song

Franz Behr, Op. 575, No. 1

42838 Cx

In May

Franz Behr, Op. 575, No. 2

Allegretto

Piano

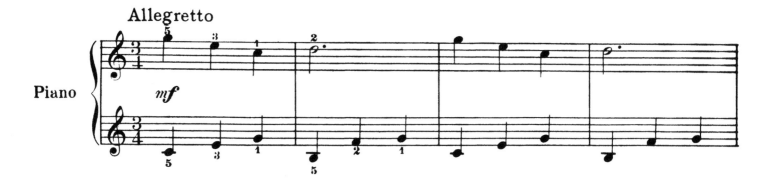

42838

Cradle Song

Johannes Brahms
Arranged by Pietro Ballatore

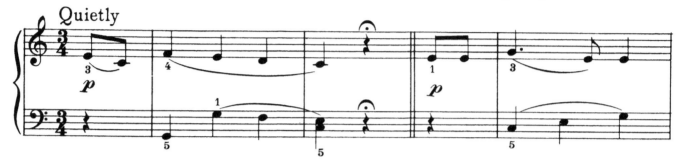

42838

Home on the Range

Cowboy Song
Arranged by Pietro Ballatore

42838

To Janet Breitenbach

Singing Bells

Long, long ago, the chimes and bells
Did learn the art of singing
  Sweet songs, and sad,
  Gay songs, and glad,
Oh, don't you hear them ringing?

Marie Seuel-Holst, Op. 21, No. 1

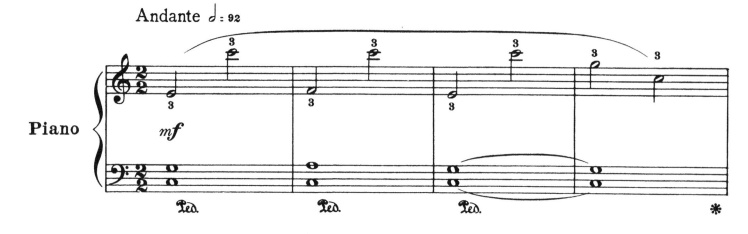

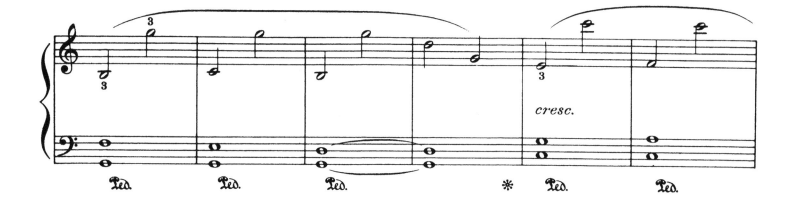

42838

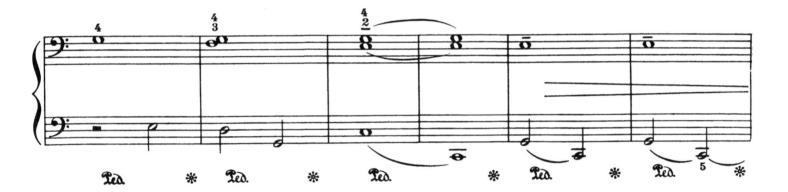

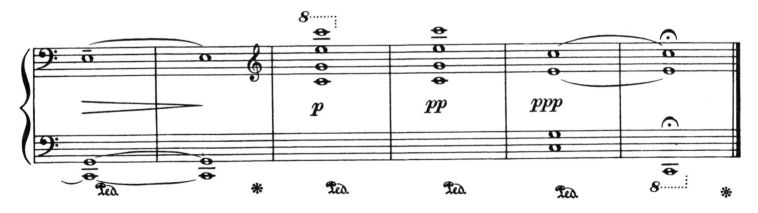

Home, Sweet Home

Sir Henry Bishop
Arranged by Pietro Ballatore

42838

Melody in F

Anton Rubinstein
Arranged by Pietro Ballatore

Andante

Dal 𝄋 al Fine

42838

Short'nin' Bread

Traditional American Folksong
Arranged by Pietro Ballatore

Moderato

Refrain

42838

Swing Low, Sweet Chariot

Negro Spiritual
Arranged by Pietro Ballatore

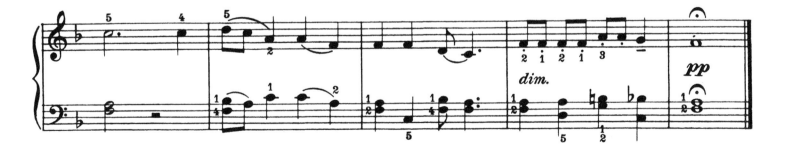

42838

Old Folks at Home

Stephen Foster
Arranged by Pietro Ballatore

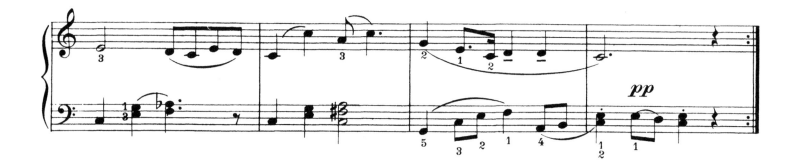

Old Black Joe

Stephen Foster
Arranged by Pietro Ballatore

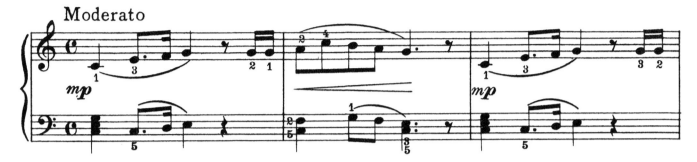

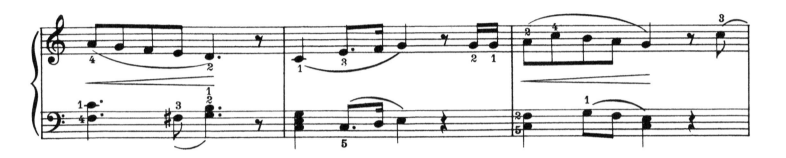

42838

Deep River

Negro Spiritual
Arranged by Pietro Ballatore

Minuet in F

Johann Sebastian Bach

42838

The Dancing Lesson

Bjarne Rolseth, Op. 39, No. 1

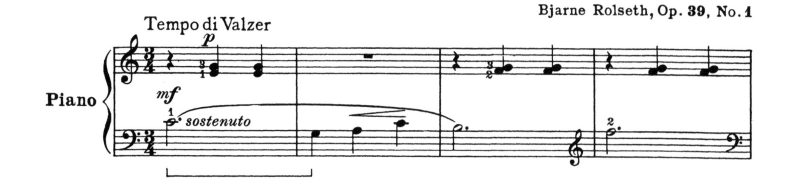

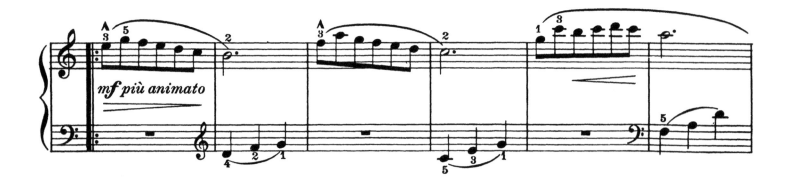

Little Fairy Waltz

Edited and fingered by
Maurice Gould

L. Streabbog, Op. 105, No. 1

Grazioso

Piano

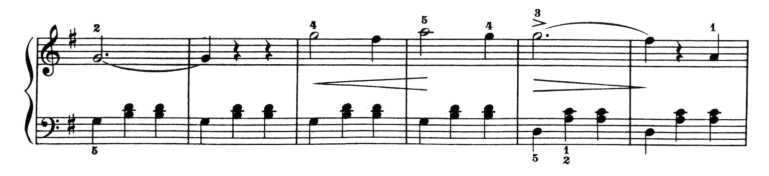

42838

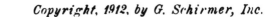

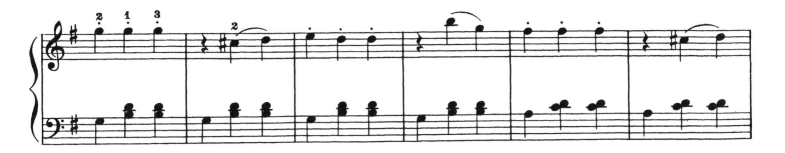

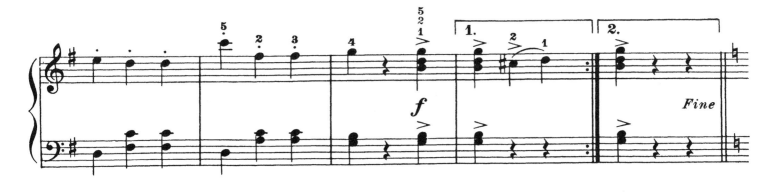

D. C.

Little Rondo in G

Ludwig van Beethoven
Arranged by Pietro Ballatore*

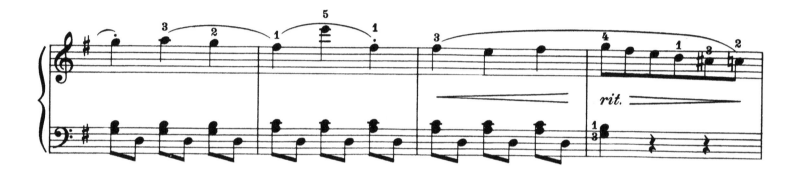

*After Beethoven's Rondo in G for piano and violin

42838

Minore

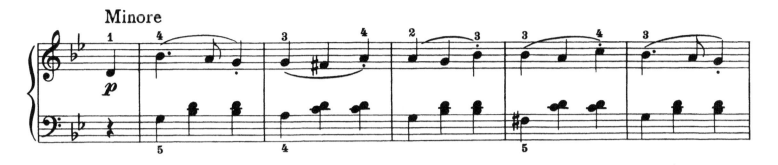

Tempo I

legato sempre

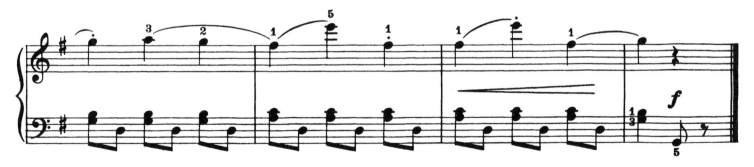

42838

Banjo Pranks

Stanford King

42838

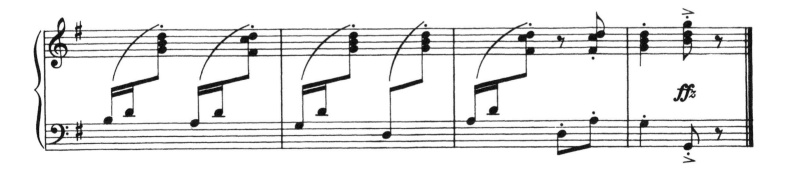

Romance

Peter Ilyitch Tchaikovsky, Op. 5
Arranged by Pietro Ballatore

42838

Teddy Bear March

Stanley E. Saxton

Like a slow March ♩ = 76

Piano

42838

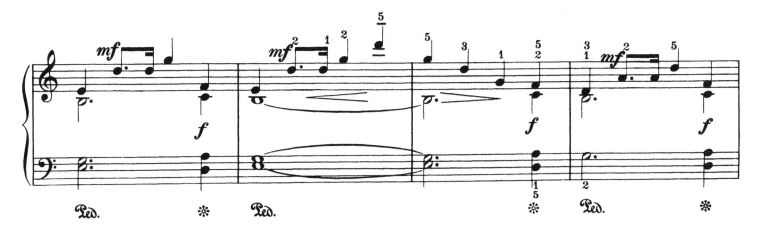

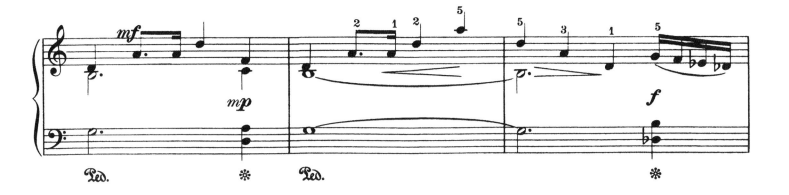

The Fair
Kirmess

Cornelius Gurlitt, Op. 101, No. 8

42838

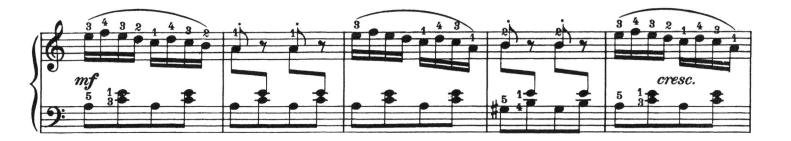

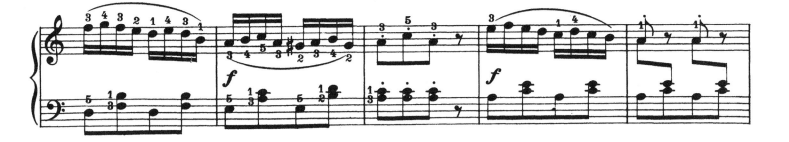

Pony Trot

Stanford King

42838

To Susan Russell

Dancing Buttercups

Elizabeth Hopson

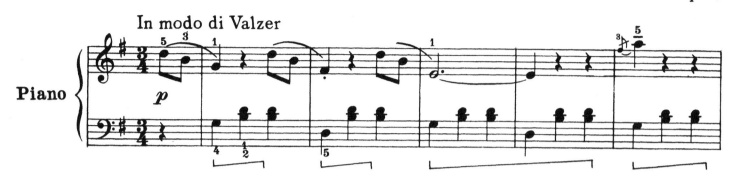

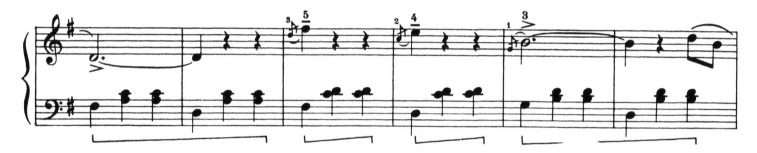

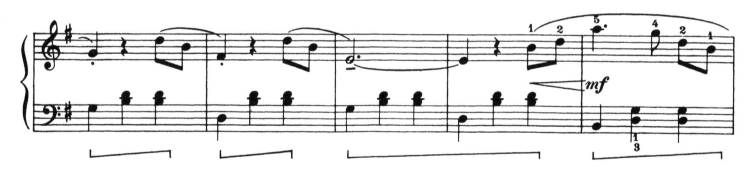

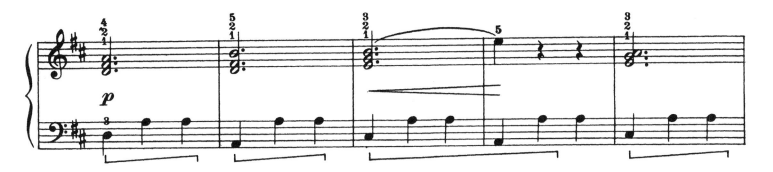

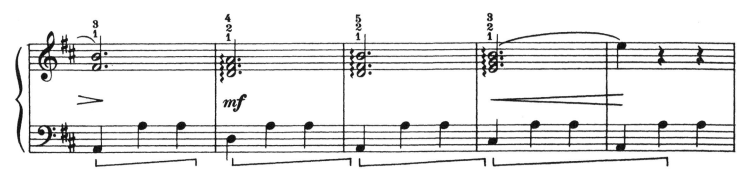

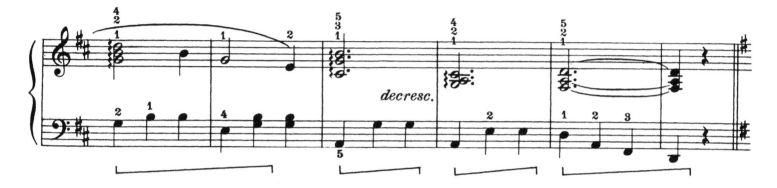

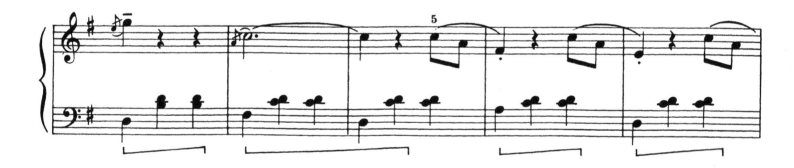

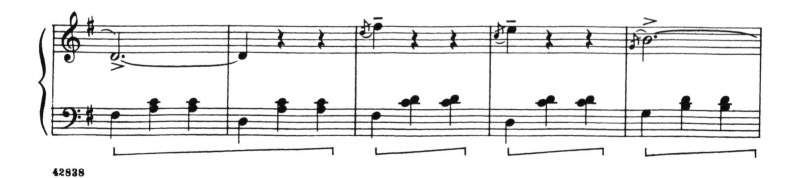

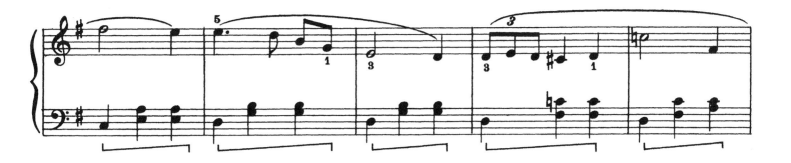

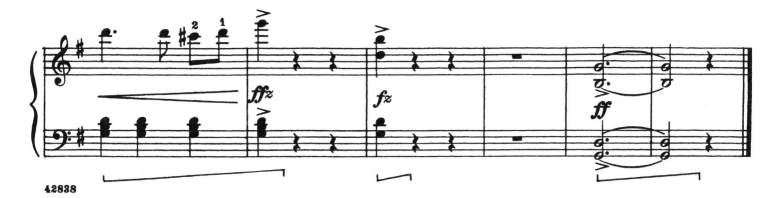

Dance from Ballet Music for "Rosamunde"

Franz Schubert
Arranged by Luis Jordá

Andantino

Piano

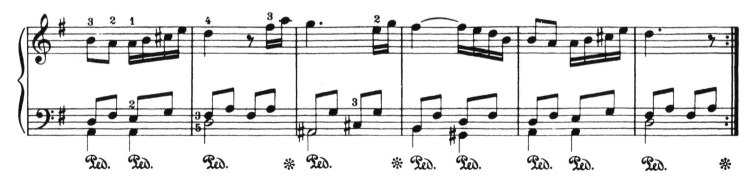

42838

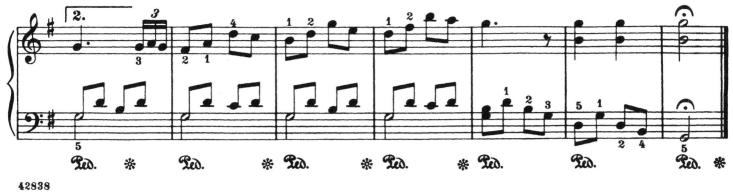

Largo

George Frideric Handel

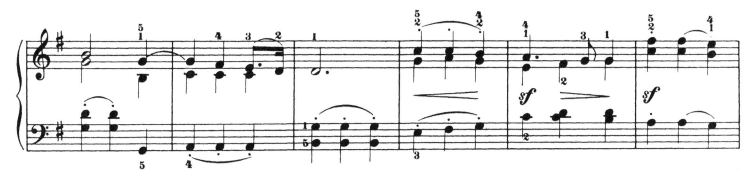

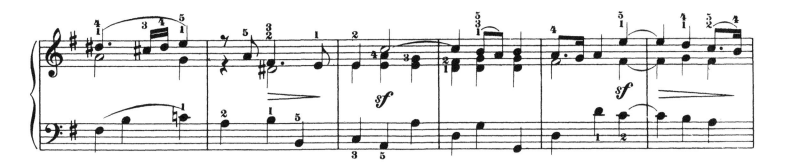

Talking it Over

William Fichandler

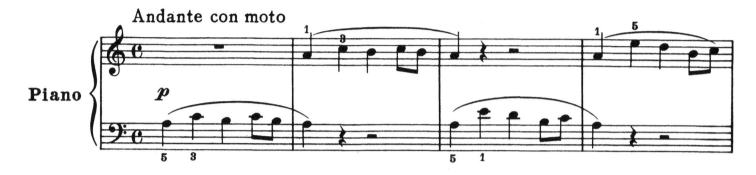

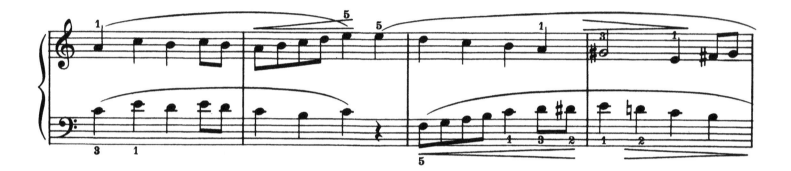

42888

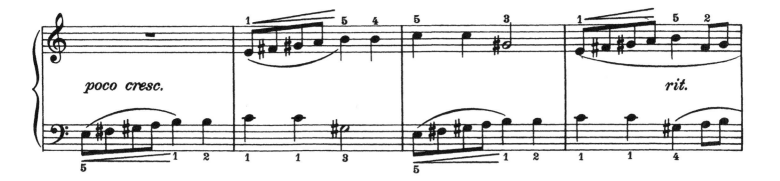

Norwegian Country Dance

Bjarne Rolseth, Op. 40, No. 8

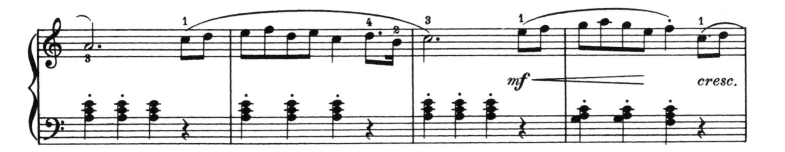

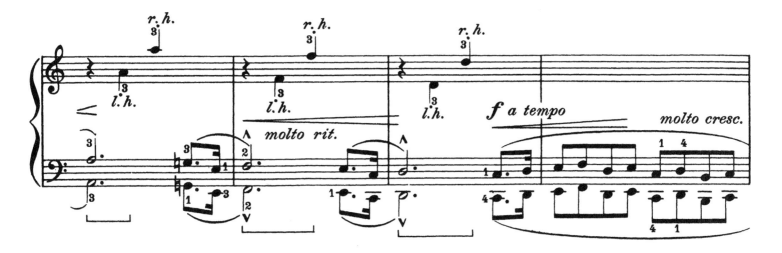

42838

Waltz

Op. 39, No. 15

Johannes Brahms
Arranged by Pietro Ballatore

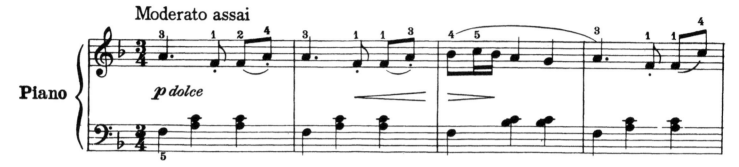

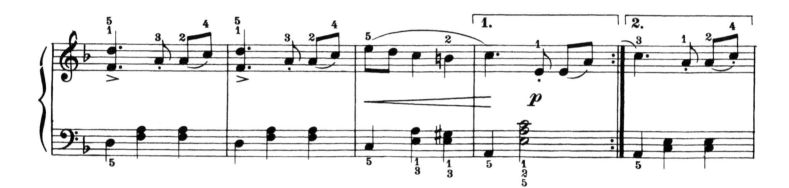

42838

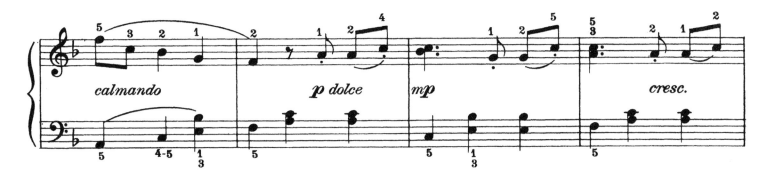

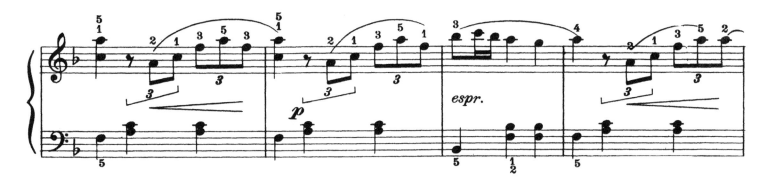

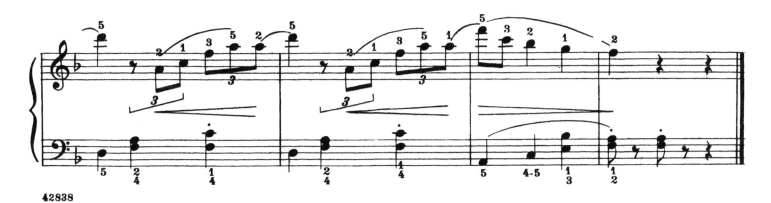

42838

Serenade

From String Quartet No. 74

Joseph Haydn

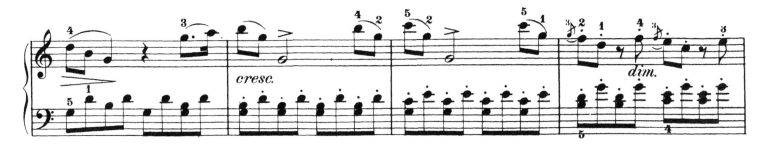

42838

The Merry Farmer

Robert Schumann
Arranged by Pietro Ballatore

Minuet

From the Opera "Don Giovanni"

Wolfgang Amadeus Mozart

Moderato

marcato il basso

42838

To Miss Helen Diemer

The Ballet-Dancer

Bjarne Rolseth, Op. 40, No. 6

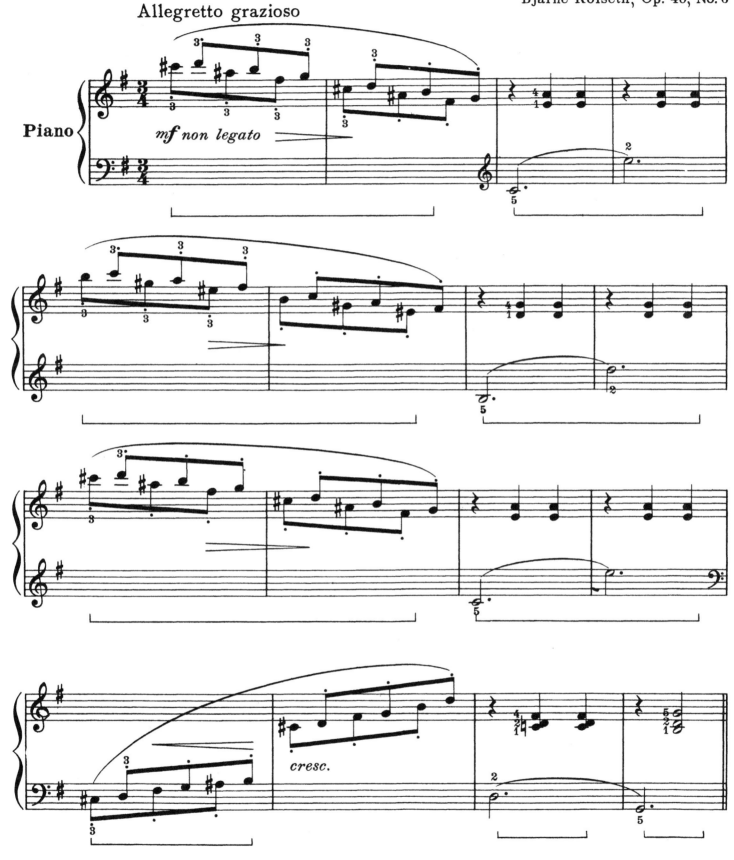

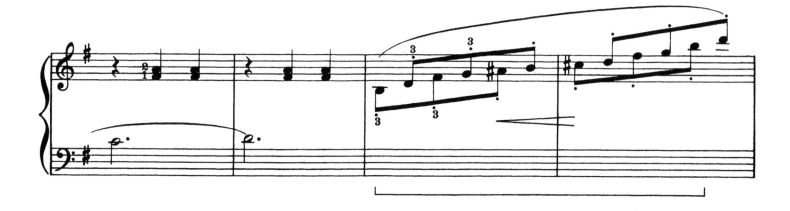

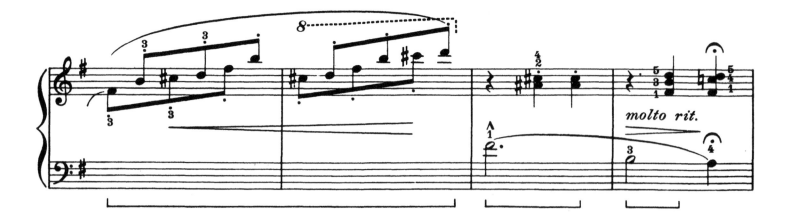

42838

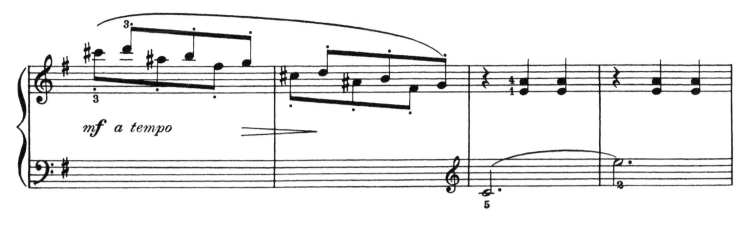

mf a tempo

cresc.

With Flying Colors

March

Stanford King

Turkey in the Straw

American Folksong
Arranged by Pietro Ballatore

Carnival of Venice

Italian popular melody
of the early 19th century
Arranged by Luis Jordá

42838

Meno mosso

Poco lento

Allegretto

42838

Con moto

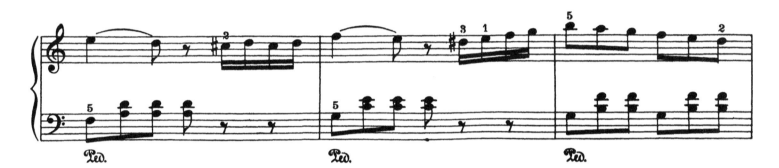

Vivo

42838

Arpeggio Waltz

Bjarne Rolseth, Op. 35, No. 4

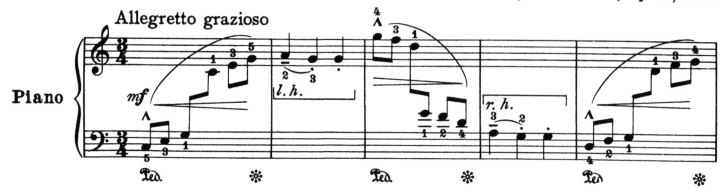

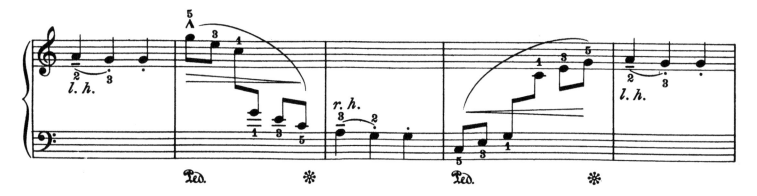

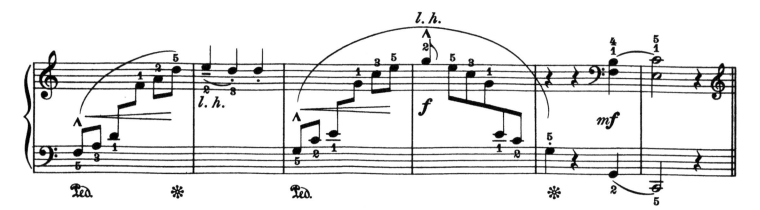

42838

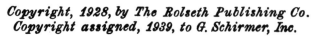

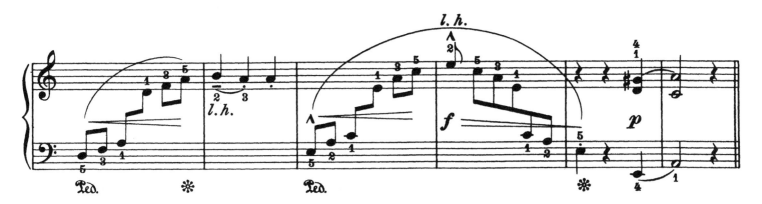

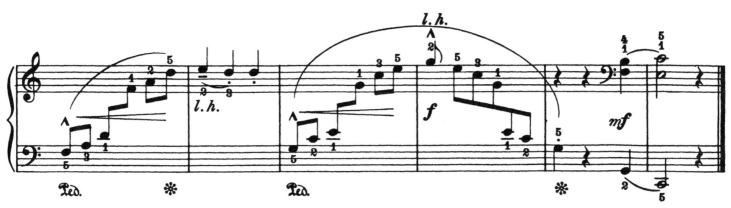

42838

Tales from the Vienna Woods

Johann Strauss
Arranged by James Palmeri

Copyright, 1947, by G. Schirmer, Inc.

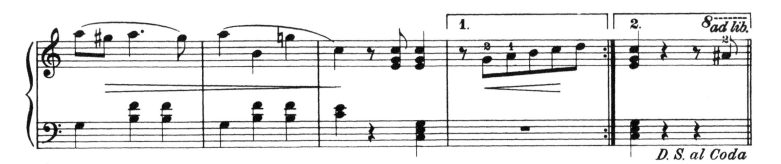

Coda

Old Cowboy Trail

Margaret Wigham

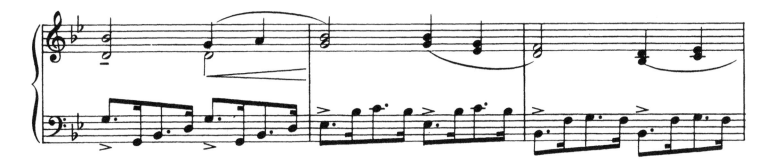

The Three Trolls

Words and Music by
Maxwell Eckstein

Three trolls at midnight
Went for a walk,
And, while a-strolling,
Started to talk.

They spoke of the moon
And the stars and the trees;
Then they all danced
In the whispering breeze.

But now trolls must go—
'Tis a quarter past three,
And the moon soon will sink
Neath the cottonwood tree.

42838

To Gloria

In a Sailboat

Olive P. Endres

42838

Wood Magic

Bernice Cougill

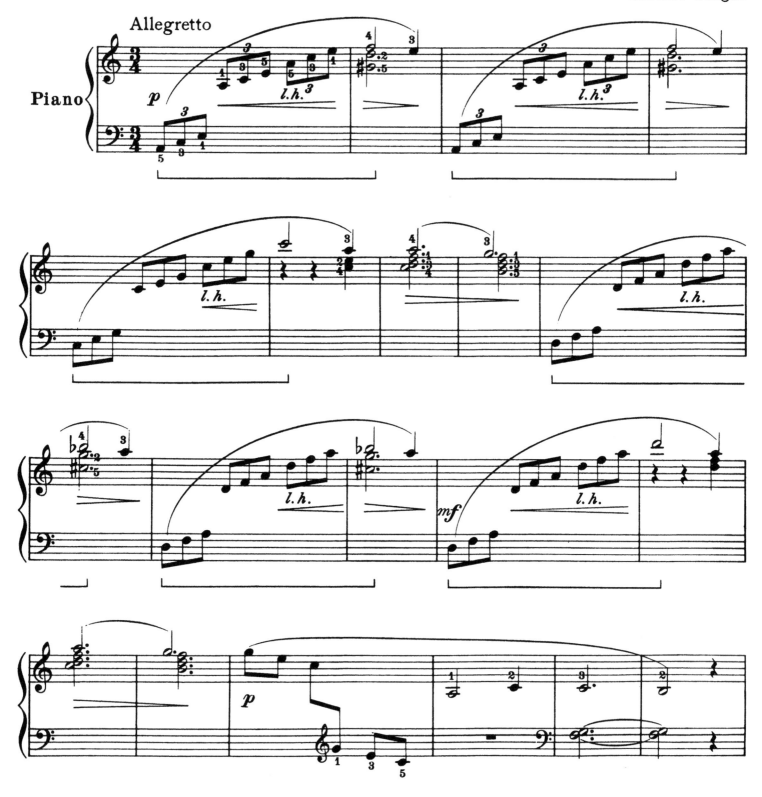

Copyright, 1932, by G. Schirmer, Inc.
International Copyright Secured

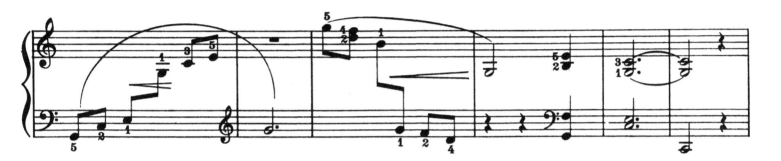

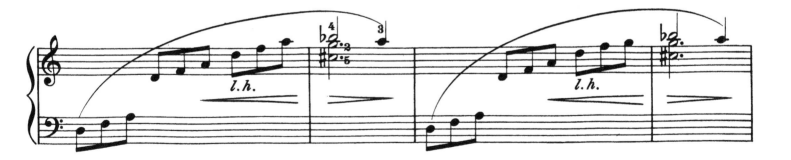

42838

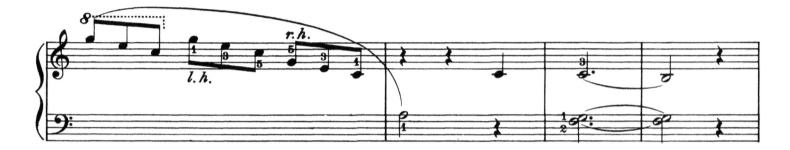

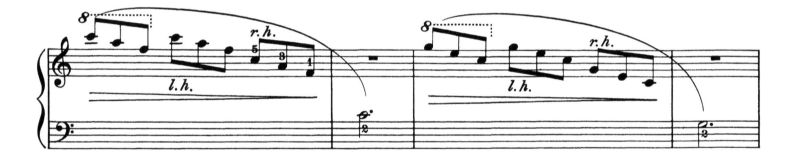

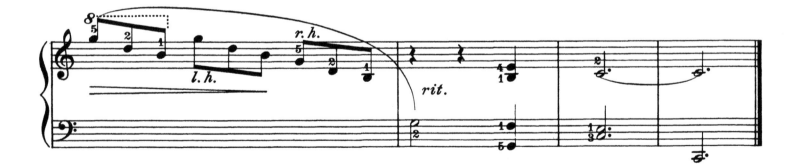

42838

Träumerei

Robert Schumann
Arranged by Pietro Ballatore

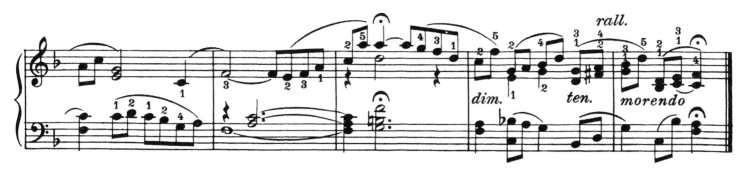

Turkish March

Woifgang Amadeus Mozart

Allegretto

Fine

42838

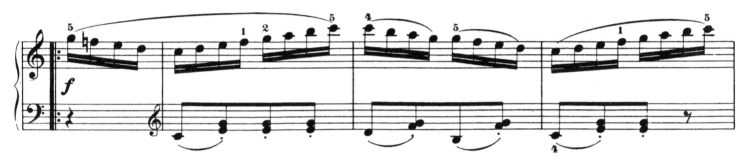

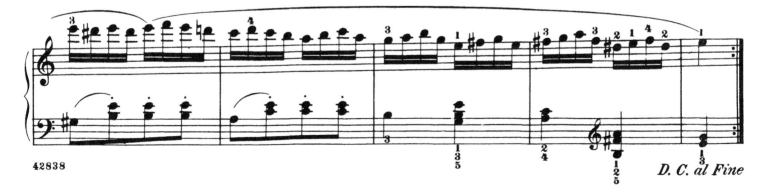

42838

D. C. al Fine

Liebestraum No. 3

Franz Liszt
Arranged by Juan Jaume

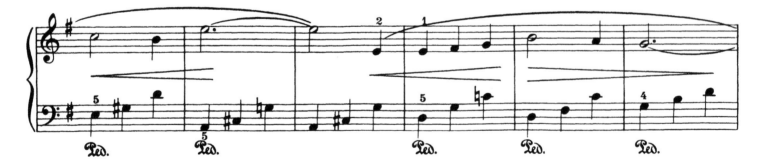

42838

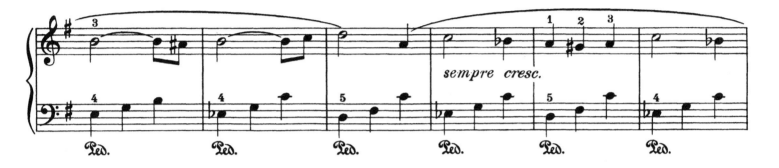

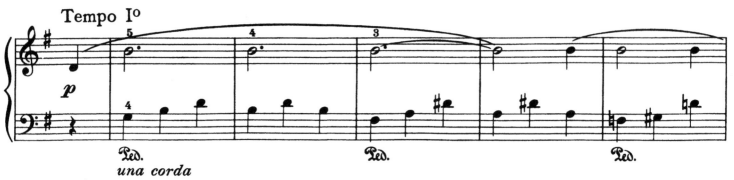

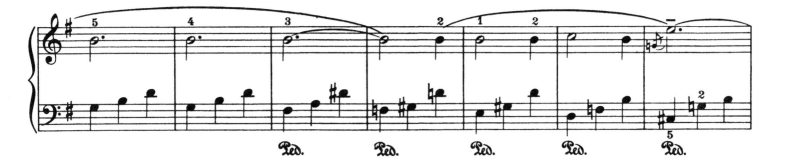

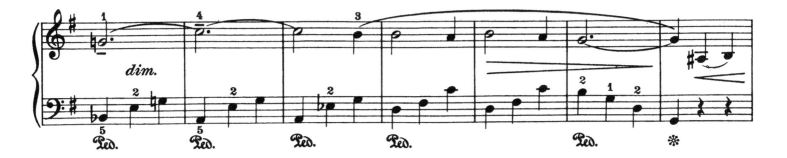

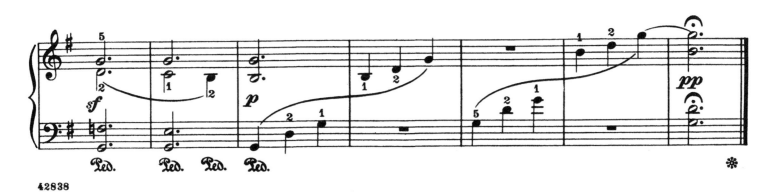

Three-and-Twenty Pirates

Grim pirates sailed, long, long ago,
And they were bold a-plenty,
Oh, ship at sea,
Beware of three
And other pirates twenty.

Marie Seuel-Holst, Op. 21, No. 5

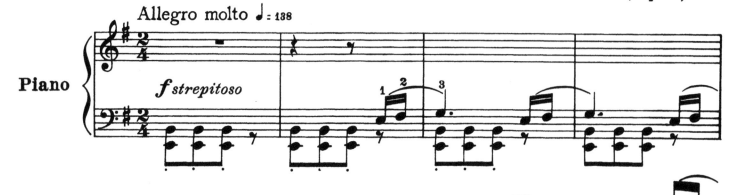

42838

Lento

Come prima

42838

Song Without Words

Consolation

Felix Mendelssohn

Adagio non troppo ♩ = 84

Pizzicato Polka

Johann Strauss
Arranged by James Palmeri

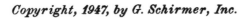

Copyright, 1947, by G. Schirmer, Inc.

D. C. al Coda

Coda

To Geraldine

Singing Birds

Olive P. Endres

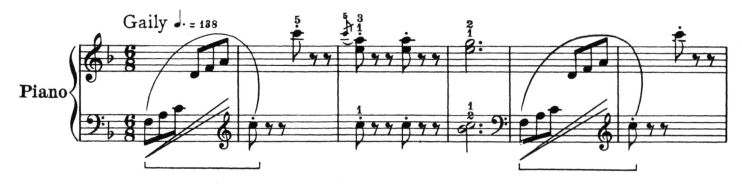

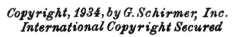

42838

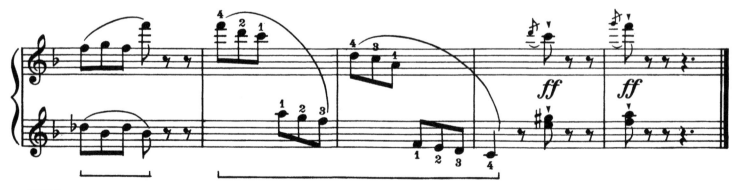

Nocturne
Op. 9, No. 2

Frédéric Chopin
Arranged by Luis Jordá

Andante con moto

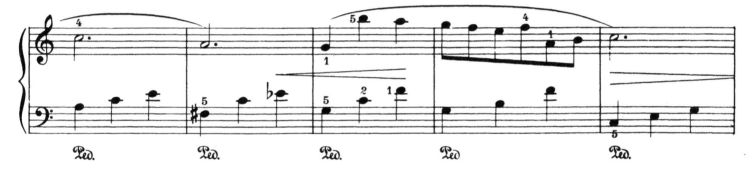

42838

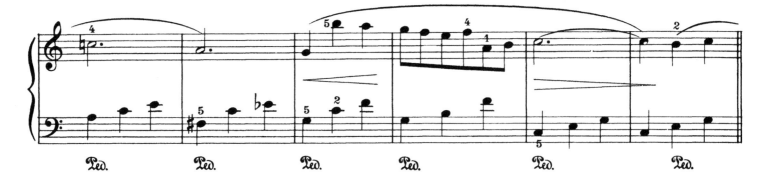

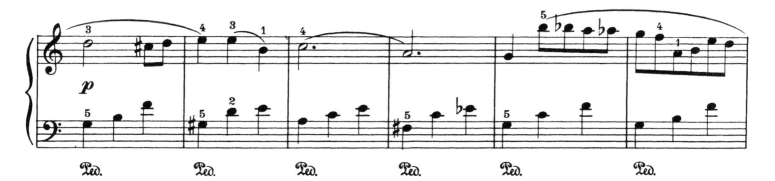

Sarabande

George Frideric Handel
Edited and fingered by
Hans von Bülow

Variation I

Variation II

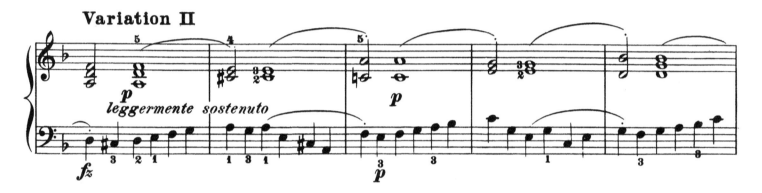

Cantabile
from "Fantaisie-Impromptu"

Frédéric Chopin, Op.66
Arranged by Luis Jordá

Piano

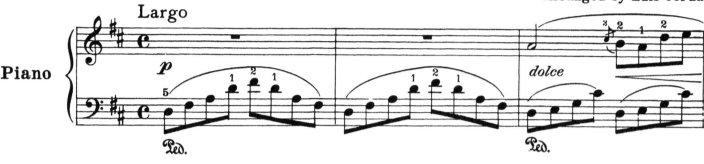

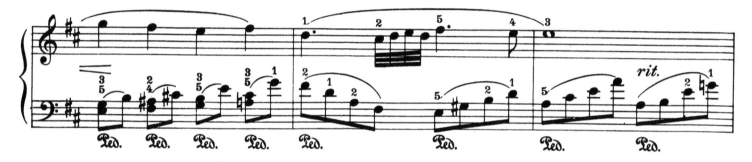

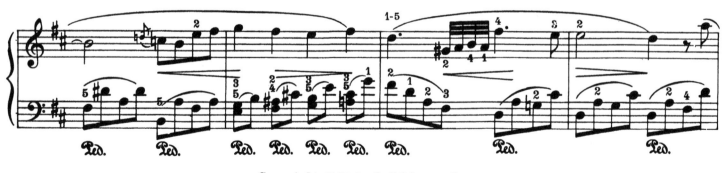

42838

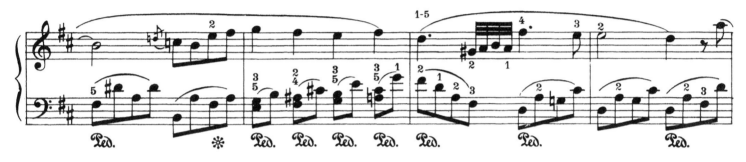

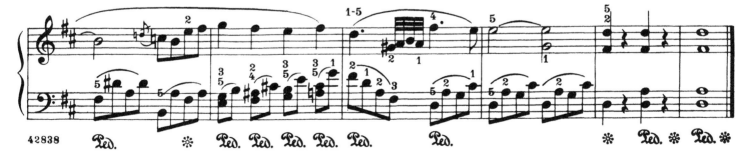

Valse Brillante
Op. 18, No.1

Frédéric Chopin
Arranged by Luis Jordá

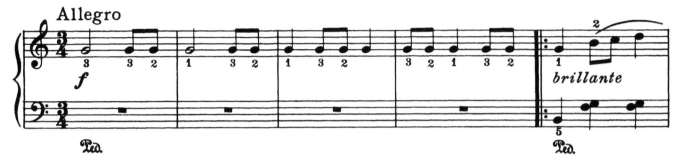

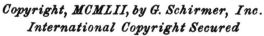

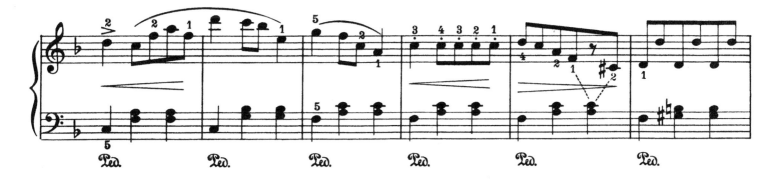

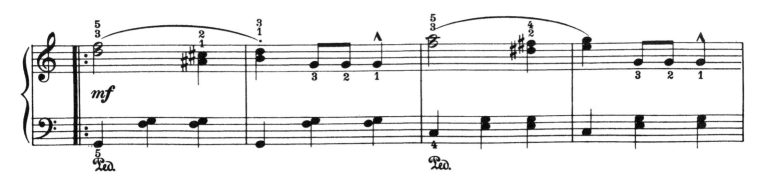

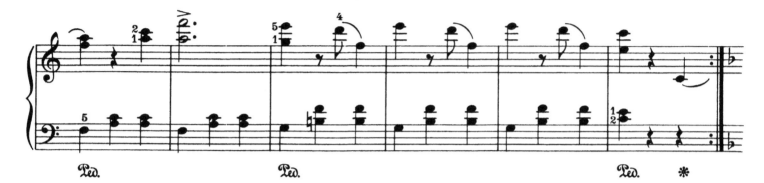

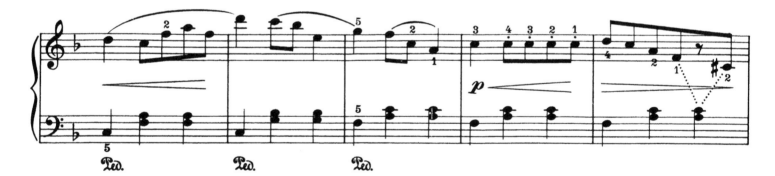

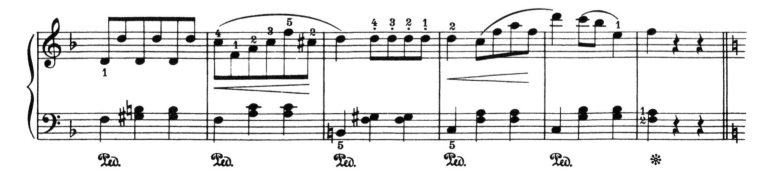

42838

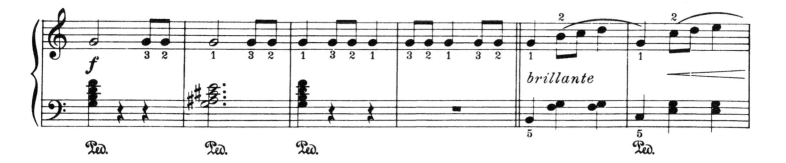

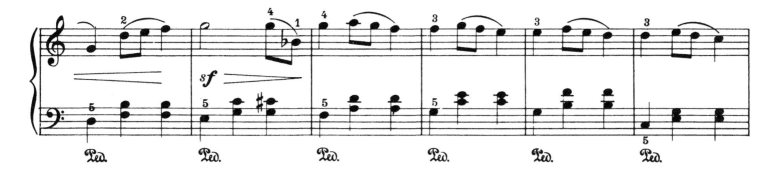

42838

Minuet in G

Edited and fingered by
Carl Deis

Ludwig van Beethoven

42838

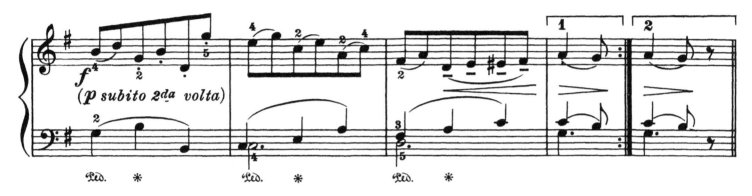

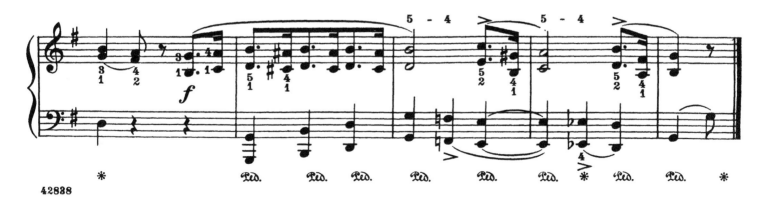

42838

Military Polonaise

Frédéric Chopin, Op. 40, No. 1
Simplified version by Pietro Ballatore

Allegro con brio

Piano

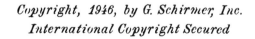

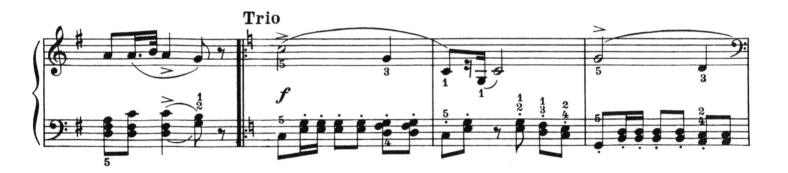

Trio

Nocturne
Op. 19, No. 4

Peter Ilyitch Tchaikovsky
Arranged by Luis Jordá

42838

Più mosso

Come prima

dolce cantabile

Hungarian Dance No. 6

Johannes Brahms
Arranged by Luis Jordá

Lento pesante

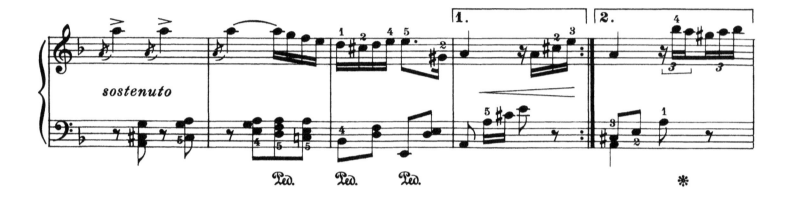

Allegro

Waltz of the Flowers

From The "Nutcracker" Suite

Peter Ilyitch Tchaikovsky
Arranged by James Palmeri

Piano

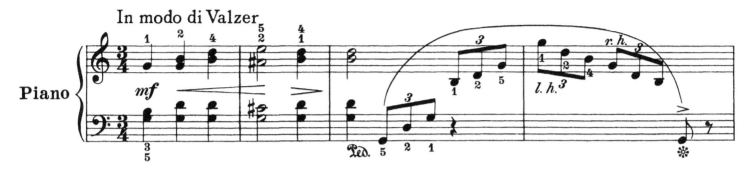

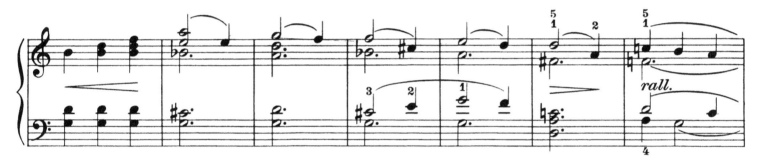

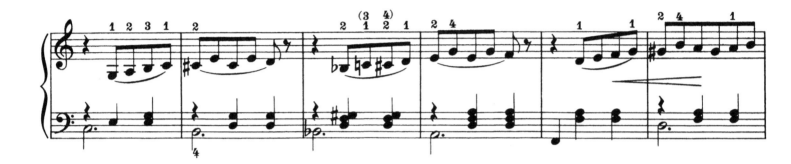

42838

42838

Marche Slave
Slavic March

Peter Ilyitch Tchaikovsky, Op. 31
Arranged by
James Palmeri

Piano

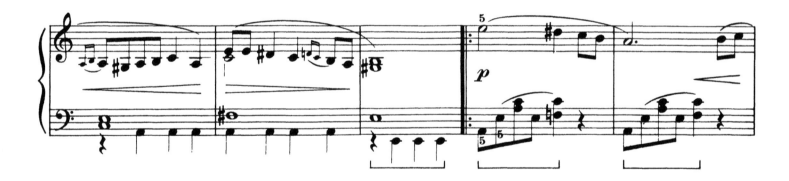

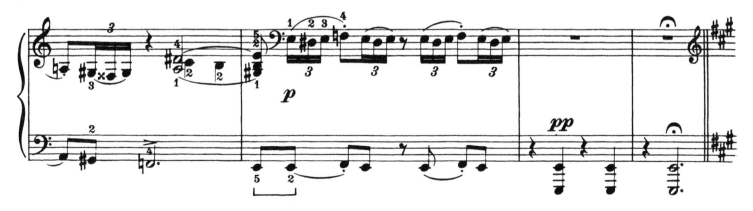

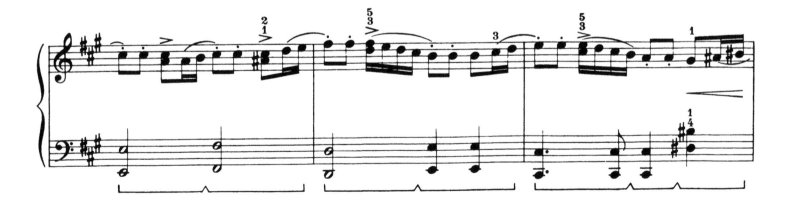